To Eled
with

Romani & Dave

C000170647

The Painter's House
Jo Slade

salmonpoetry

Published in 2013 by
Salmon Poetry
Cliffs of Moher, County Clare, Ireland
Website: www.salmonpoetry.com
Email: info@salmonpoetry.com

ISBN 978-1-908836-27-4

COVER ARTWORK: *Jo Slade*
COVER DESIGN & TYPESETTING: *Siobhán Hutson*

Printed in Ireland by Sprint Print

Salmon Poetry gratefully acknowledges the support of The Arts Council.

For Tim and Pete

Acknowledgements

My thanks to the editors of the following publications in which some of these poems, or earlier versions of them first appeared:
The Clifden Arts Anthology 2007 (Clifden Community Arts Week); *An Sionnach: A Journal of Literature, Culture & the Arts*, Vol 4. No.1 (USA, 2008); *Salmon – A Journey in Poetry 1981-2007*, ed. Jessie Lendennie (Salmon Poetry, 2008); *Orbis International Literary Journal* No. 148 (UK); *Poetry Ireland Review* No.90; *Landing Places: Immigrant Poets in Ireland* (Dedalus Press 2010); *The Stony Thursday Book*, A Collection of Contemporary Poetry, Numbers 5, 6, 7, 8, 9 & 10 (2006-2011); *The Bridge Community Journal* (Killaloe & Ballina, Co.Clare); *Southword Literary Journal* No.17 (Munster Literature Centre); *Verge*, No.1 Vol.1; *A Journal of Art & Culture* (Galway); *Cyphers* No. 69 (2010); Programme notes for Dagda Dance Company's 'Limerick Trilogy'; www.ventilatorbesed.com (Poems in Translation); *Circus Europe: Poetry and Images*, An international collaboration with Dutch Artist, Machteld van Buren and Selected Poets (Salmon Poetry, 2013); *Southword Literary Journal* No 24 (Munster Literature Centre, 2013); *Femmes d'Irlande en Poésie* (Editions Caractères, Paris, 2013); *The Stinging Fly* (2013); *The Lighter Craft* (Astrolabe Press, 2013).

The sequence of poems 'The Artist's Room' was published as a chapbook *The Artist's Room* by Pighog Press (Brighton, 2010). This sequence of poems draws on Sue Roe's biography *Gwen John: A Life* (London: Vintage, 2002) and on *Gwen John: Letters and Notebooks*, ed. Ceridwen Lloyde-Morgan (London: Tate Publishing, 2004). The title 'Mysteries of the Heart' is taken from Andre Lhote, *Figure Painting*, trans. W.J.Strachen (London: A. Zwemmer,1953, p.6. First published, Paris: Editions Floury, 1950).

Grateful thanks to Helen Carey and Sheila Praschke, past and present directors of the Centre Culturel des Irlandais, Paris and all those working there, where I was Poet-in-Residence during the winter of 2007. Many of these poems were inspired by my time there.

Many thanks to Culture Ireland for a travel bursary in 2010 that supported the work.

Thanks also to my family and friends who are always a source of inspiration and encouragement. To those who gave close reading of and responded generously to my work, heartfelt thanks.

Contents

Burying the Bulbs

The Picture of Inkbrush

Today

Time-Piece

Time-Piece

In memory of my great-grandfather, Joseph Wangler

In the wardrobe of my belonging
is a bearskin coat.
I've never worn it.
I must remember to take it out
have it altered to fit —
take a walk with the bear on my back.

I'd like to find him inside it
my great-grandfather.
The clock wound back
so I could see him as he was —
his nimble fingers placing the pins
his musical ear timing the cogs
his eye like a moon in the ocular.

I'd like to walk across Europe
to Feldberg and climb to the top,
sit with him looking out
on a snowy vista.
We'd talk about time and the clocks
he made and why he left
the house by the lake.

Why he never went back
why his bearskin coat
hangs in my house —
a ghost of truth
no one speaks about.
Is his the mark on my poet face —
why I'm always a stranger
from an other place?

Leaving

Porthole to an ocean.
One child doesn't want to go
he's throwing up
has locked the cabin door
says he'll smash the glass.

She takes him on her lap –
holds him…
the ship wrenches from the pier.
They're staring out –
someone's waving.

"Look Mam the pier is moving."
She holds him tight.
They're disappearing.
Home's back there –
it's where we're leaving.

Winter 1963

He looked so beautiful
skating the lake
making a huge figure eight.

It might have been
this time of year, late January.
I remember white
as far as my eyes could see
from the back of our old
black Austin Cambridge.

I can hear my mother say,
"Peter it's been snowing all day,
do you think we should risk it ?"

We went anyway,
his skates packed in the boot
and a makeshift sleigh.

I remember coloured lights
flickering and everyone laughing,
Lough Gur glistened
in the winter gloom.

Then he glided onto the ice –
my Da like a ballet dancer
and Mam giggled
as his dark form looped
and veered away.

He was gone, lost
in a white world as it was then,
until the moon rose
and made him visible again.

The Handyman's Daughter

I've come to a different space –
even so
my head holds the old tools in place.
In one corner hammers and nails
and hanging from a hook
a chain that looks new, untouched.

It's a bright place.
Light fills it at noon and again in the evening.
I've made space for myself –
a bed to sleep on, a table, a chair.
I like a spare, uncluttered feel.

I've laid here for days, stayed in the room
not spoken or eaten.
Then I began spring cleaning.
The first corner to clear were the tools
and books about law and rules of architecture
and a leather bound book on love.

Then I emptied out my mother's life:
a pocket stuffed with letters
jam pot covers, bottles of essence of vanilla
and ginger, recipes for puddings without sugar
and a bleached ration book.

This space is wide and generous.
The windows are always open and breezes
keep dust moving – nothing rests.
Sometimes in the evening an artist-friend visits
we sit looking at the night sky
and we talk of the planets. But no one stays.
I like it like this, the emptiness.

Daughter Lucy

Morning. Dalliance.
Time to cross over
and I was with her –
rheumy eyed from the sting.

Through the city we went
like a leg and its limp
down a lane that led to a bridge
and I was whispering
words of a bath-song to her.

The moon was up there:
a sharp pain left over
and snow fell
quiet as cotton-hair falls
from a baby's head.

I dragged her with me
her old back bent over
and sometimes the drag was immense –
except for a song she kept singing,
"Put your shoes on Lucy
we're going to the city."

The steel bridge softened with snow
our shoes covered over
our feet buried under
and her in the cark light singing,
"Show me the way to go home
show me the way to go…"

And Left Alone

IM.

Your weak heart moves through silent space
and slips beneath the sea.

                    I hear you sing in darkness.

Was it you who came or the moon reflected?

Who travelled this far so late – caused a storm
passed through what was our home

                            and left alone?

The Unknown Garden

When I look out over new grass

and smell the pungent pittosporum –

I see them.

I can tell he's there by a curl of smoke rising

and her beside him

her sapphire eyes sparkling in the early sun.

But there's a whiteness   a veil of air

that blurs my vision that I cannot wipe away

or even want to walk out into.

It's the distance I'd have to cross –

the unknown garden I'd have to walk through.

The Plum Tree   &   The Window

Something like a soul

the blossom   Like skin

Symptom of the tree   the window that I find them in

the core present.   How it seals them

                               Pressed against the pane

Round sound of absence   they strain

Plum   to see plums ripening.

Taints the heart

from where it comes.

Twine

Time is thin as string, an ancient length of measure
I found in Da's old shed,
a hair-ball he'd use with twigs
to set in straight lines a run of lettuce.

Time draws distance in and out and in
till I can touch his hand
feel its roughness, see the perfect half-moon rise
clear and pale above the cuticle of his middle finger,

intuit strength as if the image felt
and his hand in earth were a conductor,
a bridge across forbidden space –
could reach out or up from under and find me, older.

Time turns clay to pots I fill with sound
rhythms I remember, have made my own.
Hands weave together a braid of words
a bird might find, entwine her nest,
keep her warm in winter weather.

My mother is a white bloom,

she's out there –
if you don't see her I do.
You've got to watch with love
and an open heart.
She'll spot you coming in
from the dark-overgrowing.

The dead aren't cold and unbound
I've seen them folded neat as pupae
and warm in their own space.
Much as I say Death   she says Life
her white head bowed in the morning heat.

Loop

Who owns the language we speak?
Strange contortion of syllable and syntax keeps
us in the loop
of eternal conversation.

Mid-morning
sun high in the trees leaves like teeth
chattering…
I want to talk with my children
make words   listen.

Small Memory

On the Boulevard Saint Jacques, Paris

My head is a house of images –

under the eaves of my eyes swallows nest

they see me as a green tree

I am warm and safe

I feed the ones who dwell in me.

Smell

Rue Mouffetard, Paris.
IM.

"smell has the power of evocation & healing."
LOUISE BOURGEOIS

If I close my eyes I see her
if I inhale it is her skin I breathe.

The streets are cold.
I smell time it is a strange odour
an unfathomable paleness.

Wet wood smells –
some smells taste of sweetness.

Inhale the streets, the buildings
the people, the concrete, the timber,
fumes from cars and cigarettes –

perfume of thighs – profound smells.
Be profound in your existence.

Taste

The Soufflot Café, Rue Soufflot, Paris

"Art is limited but the taste of nature is unlimited."
    A CHINESE CHEF

He arrives at the same time each evening
I arrive a little earlier.
I like to watch him eat, he eats with pleasure.
He's older than he appears, older
than his dyed hair.
The waiter is attentive, familiar.

He takes a glass of red wine, swirls it round
breathes it in sips it down, slowly…
I like the way he cuts meat
the way he bites flesh, savours the taste.
He isn't handsome but he eats with pleasure.

He prefers salad to green veg, vine tomatoes
and hot peppers. Dessert is a small Tarte aux Cerises,
sweet juice wets his lips.
I drink my wine, smell warm earth inside the grape
lick my mouth, taste.

Bells

Le Collège des Irlandais, Paris

Hours pass…
sequence of trees, of shrubs, of pathways.

The courtyard is a secret
inside it everything changes.
The great doors labour against the cold,
doves scatter the stillness
their moving world careens, adjusts
seems poised on an edge.

Bells ring…time I couldn't forecast.

Song

Montmartre, Paris

Where is my reader, is she he in the world yet?
Maybe they haven't been born
maybe they are waiting with our new language
to be conceived by a woman heavy with desire?

Small fragile foetus, crimson and lavender,
your eyes float in my transparent dream.
You will be born. On that day your mother
will wrap you in the music of her river

that receives everything and keeps nothing.
You will be born and the abandoned words
will be saved, words replete with joy
words that carry tears, yours and mine –

tears for our unrequited lives.
You will be born and you will walk with the joyous.
We will sing you and me
we will be born as sister and brother.

Le Monde

Rue des Écoles, Paris

A man chants in the street —
he sits outside a café and the sound he makes
is dry as a desert.
He chants Le Monde, the world.

I hear his prayer to the sun —
a round rough sound, full of loneliness.
People who pass this way know him
they come to buy Le Monde, the world.

His voice is dark and beautiful as the elements.
In my dream we walk together
in the world's emptiness.
I want to break my silence

reach out, touch him.
He chants Le Monde, Le Monde
as cars, buses, light, air, the dead
the silent souls of all the world pass by.

Small Memory

Place de la Contrescarpe, Paris

IM.

It was midwinter.

I remember light woke me, it shone through me
made visible the fine white bones of my hands
and a criss-cross shock of red veins
gave a warm glow to the emptiness.
I walked out as if the trees, the trailing ivy
the dark soil and the timber hut were mine.

Everyday I go to her as I did once come new to her.
I arrive she smiles – she's forgotten the flotsam of her river
how I almost drowned inside her.
I sit at her window and listen –
in the stillness the music of the fountain.

She sleeps, wakes and sleeps – I touch her pale
translucent face, describe the day's pearl light
the spare trees and the fountain.
In the square below a man is sleeping
curled in a blue bag, like a baby.
People pass, snow falls…
Then the gaps, elisions, intolerant breathing.
They sleep, wake and sleep the bag man in the square
and her here, drifting inside an incubation.

I imagine them dancing –
I watch their bodies meld and glide across the square
then float high above the buildings
like lovers in a Chagall painting.
I walk out, the light is opalescent now the quiet street opens
a dog limps across my path. I feel transparent.
Windows darken and the people and the buildings –
the world moves outside them
serene and beautiful and silent.

The Eternal Garden

Jardin du Luxembourg, Paris

All forms exist in our minds –
                they have their own solidity.
Is there One form from which we all derive?
Is longing the desire to be re-formed?

Buds appear, soon it will be spring.
Secret of the azure heaven
                you breathe these white clouds
you roll them out like pearls
                from the mouth of the world.

gratitude

After the painting, The Daughters of Thespius by Gustave Moreau.
The Gustave Moreau Museum, Paris

The Daughters of Thespius waited nervously for Hercules.
Hercules killed the Nemean Lion with his bare hands
and King Thespius in gratitude offered him fifty lays
for he owned fifty daughters.

Hercules was virile more than any man –
a saviour to those who had lands and kingdoms
and were afraid of lions.
King Thespius was one such king –
an owner of wives and daughters and things.

Hercules was breathed on by fire
and he burned, his desire
was uncontrollable.
He began at seven as light faded
and finished at seven, as dawn rose.
Fifty times ecstasy is frenzy…
Hercules was in another world, briefly.
Then he fell into a deep, post-coitus sleep.

The Daughters of Thepius took the sleeping Hercules
into the wilderness. They sang to the Nemean Lion
whose body was still warm –
he hadn't yet taken his place among the stars.
He woke to their song.
He carried Hercules away. He ate the one
They called Death.

The Artist's Room

The Artist's Room

87 rue du Cherche-Midi, Paris

I looked for her in Paris…
walked from place to place, lived the smells, the sounds,
followed a plan I'd drawn, of houses, apartments,
rooms she'd lived in, that sunlight entered at a slant
and felt uneasiness –
not her presence, more an aura of hands.

Once, I thought I saw her in the Tuileries
her hair pinned beneath a hat,
a wool scarf tucked inside her coat.
She was sitting on the steps
sketching a small boy with his mother.
Wind gathered in the courtyard of the Louvre,
it swirled round the steps –
formed gusts that blew garden chairs over.
Cold air froze my breath. The Tuileries emptied.

Across the street a light went on,
a voice called out – I looked up, a figure blurred,
in half-light a hand drew the gardisette.
Distance loneliness, a figure at a window.
Someone's waiting, will he come?
She never thinks of painting –
days, months of writing letters to her love,
the space he fills, her room their enclosure,
her heart spilling over, till she feels –
'*feels*,' he says.
Till the lamp extinguishes what it reveals.

At home my easel's turned toward the attic light.
If I look out the ash tree waves its topmost branches,
sunlight floods the portrait heads.
Rilke says, '*love the corner of your room*,' its wooden floor,

its windows, the light.
What she found were small illuminations,
openings to pass through –
the self unwinding downward to the blue.

Little Interior

87 rue du Cherche-Midi, Paris

Recueillie.

Of all that's here in tones

hues dissolution −

this room is all she owns

this radiance.

'Mysteries of the Heart' 1

29 rue Terre Neuve, Meudon

Watch them, latent and deeply silent
                           as a half-formed bloom.
Something's grown
                             misshapen in the wood.

See, through the dark trees
                             bodies come together
then ease apart.
At one point, sharp sunlight splits them.

She touches him
                      in that space between them.
Her lips open.
See, he's turned away. Love is unbelievable.
What has she done ?

Look, she's holding out a hand to him –
something like torture has begun.

Drawing the Dead Leaves

'Your life can still be a work of art…'
    GWEN JOHN

She walked through the forest
'in the dark and rain, through fallen leaves'
feeling his absence, drawing on emptiness.

Rummaging, as if it were in there
the last palette of leaves.
Teaching her hand to see as the heart sees.

Learning the habit of colour :
raw umber, yellow ochre, burnt sienna.
Going deeper, darker.

Rain dripping into crevices –
études of loneliness playing the trees.

Dépôt des Marbres

Rue de l'Université, Paris

Inside, is like a spare cathedral.
Wind rattles the glass.

Talk to her about happiness.
Touch her cool breasts (*'your little Marie'*)
solitary, like an essence.

See the mulberry groove
just beneath her eye –
shadow of a fruit about to fall.

Small embryo of tears
close to the corner.

Abeyance

St. Sulpice, Paris

Watch her.
Though the day moves through her
and her through it —
her true state is suspended.

Aspirant. Some days she sits
in a state of suspension for a long time.
This is different to waiting.
Waiting is the possibility of something.
The nature of abeyance is
that nothing resolves. She understands this.

Some days she comes fully prepared
and nothing happens.
Only ends resolve. Only ends are
completely without fear.

The Whistler Muse

The Rodin Museum, Paris

Light entered from above –

she rose unravelled stretched

her feet and hands were cold

an eye twitched.

The ache of holding of being watched.

His hands moved slowly…

he held the pelvis traced the crease

that formed the round.

She stood there didn't stir

she feared a breath a word

would break the spell.

His deft fingers brushed her thigh –

he pressed a thumb just above the femur

a stream released inside her.

He caressed her smoothed her skin

tracked the spine the wide shoulders

he touched her breasts.

She breathed deeply…

the room flushed.

He felt her – extinguish.

'Mysteries of the Heart' II

Rodin's Studio. Villa des Brillants

He knew how it would be
removing the cloak from something there
and wind moving round her
and the marble stars keeping her near
                    (in his tenderness.)
Keeping her in the complex shadow.
Like an argument in his mind –
                    a falseness in her prayer.
He knew from the first whisper.

Then, silence in his cathedral, as if
                    she'd never been there.
As if, he'd seen her somewhere –
from a train window, trees moving,
                    everything moving.
Where had he seen her?
From the door of a dream that woke her
suddenly, into winter?

Last Letter

Near the end of night I looked
at my form reflected I looked at my my face
the pale flesh, the wide eyes solemn and calm.
I thought, tonight I will write it down.
I should have written last winter
when the ground was hard and cold
and trees' dark shadows lay
like oblique figures on snow.
But I couldn't.

I should have sent you my heart.
I should have cut it out —
made a book of its muscular tissue.
You would have seen our names
etched on the wall of memory.
You would have felt my life beat
in your hand. Then out of love —
from a deep well of love
you would have calmed me.

I'm standing by a window in moonlight.
Already the moon wanes —
the circle of your being fades farther.
For a time the room was incandescent,
for a time the dream of your silence
shied away. Once, I pulled from the river
the meaning of our days together.
Then you were here, poring over me.
I could feel you
you were light where I bathed.

I'm watching a man and a woman walk together.
The space between them grows —
cold enters the atmosphere.

I want to impose a sentence on them —
lock them in words forever.
Even now, I think of you as a saviour.
If you come how will I know
since your body is translucent
and your hands, which you treasure,
are pale and inconsolable?

The Still Room

The Hangar. Rue Babie Meudon.

Wind in the birch in the aspen –

all night the studio door was open.

The still room a white chair

white canvas against a white wall.

Full moon April.

She's there – asleep in the grass

cats curled at her feet

her hands stained with paint.

These nights she's elemental.

God's Artist

"To enter into Art as one enters into Religion."
  GWEN JOHN

She leaned against the timber door
and looked out across the sky.
It was winter.

She could hear a dog bark in the valley
and there was scent of fox close by.
A peregrine with beautiful markings glided above her.

Surely it is all there – the life.
Seasons come and go.
Writing in her notebook later

she thinks salvation must be elsewhere.
In a colour, or whiteness –
in the timbers' weathered paleness.

Early Light

Rue Babie Meudon

The roof opens

the sky is speckled green.

She can tell by the wind

which way light comes

slow and transparent –

until the tops of trees turn blue.

Sun bathes her face.

A space widens

that grace might fill –

doubt slips an edge.

A whiff of pigment

an overwhelming silence.

The Last of the Weather

"a seer of strange beauties, a teller of harmonies.."
    GWEN JOHN

The painter boarded a train for Dieppe.
It was September, the air was cool.
An image from a dream stayed with her
of a coastal town, a beach to wander.
Chloe had written earlier of wind on the sea
how it rippled the surface and light caught inside
made it translucent, cinereous, silver.
The night before, sitting at a brasserie in Paris
she heard the news : France and Germany were at war.
She felt lonely, confused.
In the same letter, 'I'm sending an almond tree'
its blossom will cheer you.

She sat by a window and slept awkwardly,
the tilt of the train, its monotony, lulled her.
Sounds floated : waves, gulls, westerlies.
Thin souls conjured from cloud drifted landward.
The world changed –
filtered through the particular, it diffused,
became tones, shades, volume, space.
She wrote in her notebook : Stages of decay.
A colour memory. Hint of blue.
Heart's dried pigment – white dust
sifting, formless and indistinct.

Time of day and seasons. Her mother sitting
on a beach. Wind sweeping up sand.
The child-painter watching from a cliff,
her sketchbook tied with a strap,
a pocket of pencil, her hat blown back.
Her eyes held by the glare, intent on the mystery.

The painter painted the last of the weather
and made her way to the sea. She stood on the shoreline.
Birds flew in the clouds, dark spots moved on the water.
Waves broke round her feet.

Thunder sounded…it's over Broad Haven, she thought,
Bride's Bay in darkness, rocks daubed with rain
a smell of iodine and salt corrosion.
She glimpsed the light, its strangeness and wonder.
She felt changes of colour, subtleties of tone
each of the other everything seeping together
making the world seemless, complete.
A small boat drifted in, a toy she'd hand painted
and set on the sea a long time ago,
a craft someone might find and climb into.

The Painter

Gwen John to Marlene Dumas

Indelible heart

fades beneath the skin

but not.

Baby hands

dipped at birth

drip colour out.

The snow its pure untouched

becomes a trail of wound –

a creature strayed

a winter bitch

a wolf perhaps.

Burying the Bulbs

Becoming

For Amy and Shane

In the slow, unfolding dawn think about who you are
                                    who you will become.
Then let it go, breathe it out
                            before it grows indistinguishable
from the million thoughts that crowd your mind.
These bright days watch the sky's infinite drift
                                it casts a shadow where you sit.

Time between this and that
                        time processing the dawn as if earth
and sky were weights borne in, squeezing life from a dry raiment.
Neither here nor there
                        these days that bridge time suspended.

February –
grass waits, bulbs wait, everything caught
                        between becoming and its own ending.
The same wonder or fear
                        depending which way light enters on any day
and you walk the road attentive –
something unwinds, is unwinding round you:
a blurred edged phenomena, a smudge
                        a watercolour rending of our world
this space we live in, this breathable dimension.

This is my wisdom, these halcyon days
                            the light shy guest of morning
brightening the curtains and I lie
                            imagining snow outside the window
my love sleeping, doves cooing in the trees
a murmurous incantation   plucks the heart   sounds of loss
looming in mid-shade, in silence.
And we wait
            between love's first light: a mother's face
                            and who we are becoming
on this day, in this place.

April Morning

For Agnes

Remember the beautiful words,
in the morning,
in the early quiet of the day.

It's joy you recall of seeing
and hearing, of knowing you belong here,
in this late April blooming.

This morning will never come again,
not these colours, nor the sky
hazy and pale, nor the cherry blossom
an iridescence waving in the distance.

So much fades into the space
between where we sit now
and the cherry tree that seems
so far away, a pointillist's impression,

a connection to the heart,
to colours suddenly present –
as the lost might be, the loved, the missing.

Listening to Trees

I remember the trees this time last year
                              how they bowed down
and I stretched to grasp their branches.

Then the wind, a wild summer wind
                              took them away from me.

I've changed since then, become more myself
though when are we whole?

Is there a time between darkness and light,
                              a space between two stars
where we stand, alone and invisible?

Midsummer, wind in the trees begins as a wave…
Whatever is out there, hear me breathe –
          my eyes like winged leaves beneath your canopy.

30° August

Sometimes in summer I long for winter.

I want to hunker down, lock myself in.
A night creature I'm ill suited to the sun –

friend to darkness, sister to the shade
I live listening, ear pressed to earth's pulse
my own imagined music

like felt notes to a deaf composer.

Burying the Bulbs

Through these burnished days these days closing round us
slowly fading I'm growing back down. I feel a rooting or re-rooting.
Mid-life a bit beyond – I don't want to see too far
there maybe nothing. Forward to the unseen unseeable
steps down into the well into cold air and no light
no blinding illumination only vague sounds echoes of voices heard
way back in my life names learned by osmosis –
shade of joy shade of brightness shade of joy.

It's begun again a gold hue glowing same dissolution same thinning
as if the world were frescoed and ancient which it is.
Light stirs in the east a swirl of wind in trees
I want to touch the leaf before it falls and the long stemmed rose
the timber wall the Budda's mildewed head the small stone pathway.
I want to turn inward become so still at the still point
I might be a stone rained on blown against.

I sit seven am almost mid autumn leaves pyramid the lawn
a reckless gathering. Every notation is a prayer –
that's how I experience the early rising.
Sitting in half light I listen a cat walks the gravel path…
I imagine a silent drift of wings. Autumn – dry leaves
cats' moulting crows calling through the morning air.

In praise of stillness – warmth wraps round me a hue an aura.
Nothing sacred about sitting here waiting for light.
I have a sense of quietness – the house empties birds fly the eaves
outside trees shed their leaves – nothing survives its own telling.
We watch and wait we move about to break the silence
the weight of being witness and words fail us.

What can I say after all the clever phrases?
Words pile against the dark a trawl of black cloth cloaks
our fear of no light at last – no last light to illuminate the fall.

All patterns all forms and language dreams and dreams not yet dreamt
drift the darkness circle the world and drop down –
breath blown from the wind's world.
Someone mutters in the dark unknown – something broods above us
and understands the world within the world
the inside-out upside-down of it. The sky of all I know remains elusive.

Reading words like a gospel or a balm taking succour from the lilt
the drop the drown of them – I search a book to find a little poem
a canticle of verses mother rhymes all are songs of autumn.
Sun – a relief of light through the front window
the early world's a mesh of music a neighbour's dog barks a car passes
the world wakes – things re-emerge in faith.
We are the world is unreasonable the sadness is we learn too late
to flow or float inside it – to simply breathe the sumptuous light.

With becoming comes winter all time leans that way.
October burrows under half hides its face a veil drawn
like someone dear that you remember
someone you whispered last words to in this life.
Across pluvial plains early pearl of water things pile together
trees grass fences – last glimpse of eyes sinking down
winter's flood rising – as was written once as the story goes…
Caught in gale force winds a dove hovers unable
to go forward or return.

Odour of winter hail on gravel a gust in trees – wind comforter friend
this instant is real only this remains. Leave the known path turn west
to the pine wood there's a small grove of dead grass
an almost perfect circle the sun never reaches
but as it drops at evening a pale light washed through with gold
transforms the grass – stand inside it push through
the kingdom of pine needles to be disassembled.
See how you've changed how simple your life seems.

Make a way as you said you would no need to know the destination
here's a good place to begin – listen the air is singing
the sky is lavender and pink. Here's a place a moth furled into
and later unfurled different – wings twitch a seldom breath
mimicry of bark its small heart hidden. It is deeply away that place
but I know it – a bell sounds white light of morning
yellow zest resurgence. We come again at least become
what we were then – ovum pod light hidden inside the tender self.

November Day

For Joan McKearnan

3am

Then, there is prayer.
The act of praying, of being inside the tree
and kneeling down inside the tree.
Of being still as a still pond
and being inside the pond.
Lying down with water in prayer.
Then there is the habit of rhythm
body seconds, 0.9 of a second
pumping the prayer
and there's a bowing down inside the body
of prayer, being inside life
as prayer. Being there.

1.40pm

Birds lift from the wet earth
unfurl into cloud, soar across the sky
and I wonder if I wait here will wind lift me
carry me as light above the land ?

5.15pm

Evening light creeps in.
Shadows spread across the paving.

A wren pulls cotton
from a rag hanging by the studio door
and that long shadow is not my son
but a trees arm spreading,

slipping into his body with a familiar sway.

For a second I see him out there
against the weathered timber.

11.30pm

Diary Entry: *To my mother.*
Winter. Water stills.
Everything falls inward.

The well is full of stars
and the night sky
 is a constellation of swallows.

December

crunches under feet.

Snow whirls round my shoulders:

white floaters

eyes frozen with grief.

Seam-less

For Richard

Evening into night   sky white in its fading out   into its out

further than the last cloud and its lessening

visible to the end as darkness is.

The no-longer long-gone silence here –

inaudible precipitation of wonder over everything.

White rose   shade of stillness and whiteness of surface

on a page and in the sky.

 Do you hope   were you hoping as I that it would go on?

not end or begin again but indwell its duration…

this stretched-out-slim moment of summer.

Meditation

On Temporality

Not the house where you live   or how it was   but now
as you walk out
light's bright wing above the horizon.

Perfect blue   unclouded
your hand sees-through to the moon fading back at that moment.
A universe measured rounded.

The sunflower opens   waits   its seed-black centre feeding
and the present: a moment gone   in its own way nothing
without the earth
turning over and around   its slow-growing   its hunger.

No sense now of the day before   the hours prior
standing here without memory   empty   as the tree will be.
The world tilting   repeating particulars in times regular and seasons.

No final number   no chart a moment you remember when you
        were whole.
Layers peel back   the daily ongoing…backward to a beginning
the future hidden in still-dark matter.

The Picture
of Inkbrush

In a Church in Arezzo

The Church of San Francesco Arezzo.
(After the frescoes 'Legend of the True Cross' by Piero della
Francesca in the Cappella Maggiore)

The lie returns, here in this church in Arezzo –

discharged into air dizzying inside the great dome

it waits to come into brightness.

Inside a fold of keepsake what was hidden stirs.

A bird released weaved and whirled

flew blind the space, traced an arc inside the nave

then rested on a scale, where souls are weighed.

Light pierced the glass, bathed the frescoed walls

made bright the Tree its lush greenness.

The bird flew down passed the painted city to the outskirts.

Against a pale-blue sky the Tree stands luminous.

Who believes the last deceit?

There is no sky, these are not trees.

The bird sees too late and flies toward it…

Cells

*After the cell paintings by Fra Angelico
in San Marco Museum Florence.*

CELL 1. *Noli Me Tangere*

Where there's no going
or coming
No coming from
or to
No knowing who

CELL 2. *Deposition*

The mother herself was
and the son
Their blood ran in rivulets
down the wood
made its way back
as blood does

CELL 3. *The Annunciation*

Sublime beauty
the shock of it
the suddenness
And her frail as a lily
pale as pigment
doused in snow

What came in
by a curve of light
formed unbeknownst
out of bare brightness?

CELL 6. *Transfiguration*

A keystone holds the arc
in place
like the heart
axis of our fate

Arc perfects a curve
holds him
in its embrace

The self and he
were once
more beautiful
than One could be
Beauty is the mystery

CELL 7. *The Mockery of Christ.*

1
A hand slipped inside the fold
cold fingered the heart
made it sore
Who follows knows
What's more
hearts harden
turn taunt as before.

2
Trust no-one
if their feet don't leave a trace
if their eyes don't smart
from the sting of grace

CELL 9. *The Coronation*

Her skin's taut silk shivers
Pearl wings
white light luminous
moon diaphanous

CELL 10. *The Crucifixion*

Where lines meet
blur or disappear
or parts of
erase over years
a space brightens
A Way opens
It is over he said
and glimpsed the vastness

The Handmaid's Tale

Annunciation to Anna

From the frescoes, Scenes from the Life of the Virgin by Giotto
The Scrovegni Chapel, Padua Italy.

That night I continued as I do
to spin the mistress told me a lovely wool.
Seated outside her chamber I listened to her pray.
The room was dull – a glum green like yew trees.
Age has made her grey.

I heard her say His name over and over –
then silence, a cloak to quiet her.
Was it one or two voices I heard, whispers
a litany of words, a secret perhaps?
That night where she knelt glowed
like a fire inside her chamber
as if light leaked through a star
the floor a flood of silver.

Later she said an angel came –
pushed in through the arc above her.
I thought the rightness of it
that one with wings would come
made for air and drift he'd fit
a swift through a small arc hand outstretched.
"A birth" she said.
From that day her eyes were clear
and she sings a larkspur to relieve her joy.

Oh that one might break this seamless skin
or I like her become grey and spend
my days in silent prayer.
In faith my celerity and grace as I climb the hill
behind my mistress' house is such
that I no longer pray though long to fly
into dense consistency of stars and sky.

Passagio

Museo Morandi Bologna, Italy.

Landscape's where I lay down
spread like Morandi's lush brush, arms wide
eyes caught in the downward thrust of shade
the passage of light from inception to infinity.

Evening thins to grey, shadows drift westward.
When soul speaks what does it say?
I keep asking the question keep interrupting the day
on its thread of blue air.

Where light lays the world widens –
mine is widest here, under these trees
beneath these spare branches.

The Picture of Ink Brush

A wolf holds my arm
guides my hand
dreams a new language
I must learn.

Wei Shuo whispers my name
gives me a brush made from
wolf hair and leaves –
tells me, black is insatiable.

I paint waves with filigree curves
and a boat with blue sails
and a sky with eyes
like the sun and moon.

The wolf curles to a hoop at my feet.
Wei Shuo is sleeping.
I sit at the bow of my craft
steer it out to the deep –
over the ink dark sea.

Christina's World

For Katryn and John

Buy a Day Get the Summer Free, was something I saw from
      a speeding car and jotted down.
We were driving northeast from LA, the freeway spinning
      out and flat – everything getting whiter.

It's all purchase and count, even days even seasons.
I could feel it
        the summer unrolling in the heat, in the early light.
Cars shimmery like jewels, a mirage obscuring vision.

And the landscape in the distance, the width of it
fields stretching so far
          edges become suddenly luminous, dangerous.
Like that painting by Andrew Wyeth, Christina's World,
the gold grass, the house a dark mouth yawning on a high horizon.

I was twenty. I thought Wyeth was god.
I wanted to touch his eyes, see through them.

I was thinking summer its lightness, its purity.
One long day after another
mother's voice calling us in.
Fleeting sounds: birdsong, buzzing, a lawnmower,
          like loneliness or longing.

Raspberries swollen and warm, red teeth, a shower of roses tipping
          the garden wall,
smells of fresh mint and rosemary,
windows thrown open, Joni Mitchell playing it out
        the coyote, a dead part that woke and shook,
an old witch-stick quivering its magic.

If I could raise the price of a day I'd be home and dry.
I could cut my costs in other ways, sell my future, hell I'm fifty six
                                        what comes after this?
One free summer for a day – it's which to choose
                                        how much to pay?

Shadow Procession

After the exhibition 'Five Themes' by William Kentridge
San Francisco 2009.

People leaving the country of their belonging.

A long trail of them stretching down dust roads

over dry mounds at twilight as the moon rises.

The procession unwinds, a chain of dark forms

silhouette against the sky.

Where are they going, the wounded, the disaffected ?

The line winds through darkness, into towns, onto streets

across deserts, tribes of loneliness pulling carts –

women with lamps like censers singing,

"what a friend we have in Jesus."

Black smoke rising to a charcoal smudge.

Neutral

"Insignificancies acquire great importance."
  Louise Bourgeois

Out of whiteness she came
her shadow melded to a form
a vertical paleness in a winter storm.
She grew from the light of a page
from the margins of something he'd made.
In her defence he drew a line
a significance she could ease into.
The painter construed a slight shade
a ghost-face edged with a braid
and coaxed her forward – he was curious.
He gave her a name, made her rhyme
Clara was indistinct – undefined.
She was white from the outside in, pure as titanium.
That night he was woken by screams –
deep in his sleep she'd followed
his dream to the centre.

Self Portrait

Once I discovered I would live

I spent all my time living.

Some times the world moves

too slow, my instinct is to run.

I've forgotten the door

the stalker entered by

and my prosthesis

which limb I wore it on.

When I come home to myself

I ask, what is my purpose?

Whatever I do is in me –

the wayward child is in me.

Some things come naturally.

There's only one way to be

in the world –

that's what I've become.

The Painter's House

See, a house of wood on a hill
and a small house made of tin
a cabin built of shale a house of stone
and houses of the rich
many houses built into one.
The house of this god and that
and the house of exigency where he lives
and the poor house of sin set in a wilderness.

The cliff house with waves rushing toward it
and the ghost-house that floats on the deep
and the house of sand that is disappearing.
The house of justice stands alone –
light enters by chink
among the squalid a house has no name
no number no street.
A bridge is a house of shelter for some a house
is painful to remember and there's the house
of terror that has no shape
and the ash-house you taste in your mouth.

And there's the house of the painter
and the tree that rises to greet those who enter
and there is her house within the house
which is where she sits her easel tilted
to the light and there's the painting
she makes with a house at its centre
and the nails she feels that hold it together.

The house left-alone knows a storm will come
it dreams its own destruction.
You have to live inside an empty house
to feel the wind that's blown it out.

Lonesome Big City Dweller

for David

He just popped onto my screen:
DNA, transposition of the family line, so like beauty I'm stunned.

It's true I say to myself, we love them way beyond ourselves
they make us the aspiration we once had.

I remember the first Surrealist book I bought
and the photomontage Lonesome Big City Dweller :

Bayer's large eyes staring out from open palms
and I see him, our adult son, his face inside the circuitry enclosure

fixed between two spheres, a nowhere that doesn't hold him fast
an image as fleeting as a sunbeam.

I imagine his shoulders sprout plumage I can feel the thrum
of tiny wingbeats like a fan.

We drift in and out of conversation
and I'm thinking how we slip through shapes, how we replicate:

a semblance, a word, a perspective like Bayer's ghostly
fingers fingerprinting chimeras on a building –

or a paleonthologist's find, a wing bone caught in siltstone
our fibrous strand stretching into the future

a spot so insignificant, it seems where I was is where I am –
a species lost in thought, a genus of brooding dream

not the smooth progression: stardust to his hand
waving across a vast tremulous expanse

but a double helix set to music we'll never understand.

Today

Forgiveness

After reading Allan Peterson's, On the Nature of Forgiveness

I took your floating chair and its shadow and sat in half-light reading

The Nature of Forgiveness.

Something I know about   in my own way   if it's possible after

small deaths and genocides: Syria February 2012

women and children hands tied behind their backs…

Early morning birds are up soffit to tree top

home to the determined   the heart beat at the centre

and the apple blossoms' pink nuclei

the clematis its minute by minute opening-out to light

as if it had one word to repeat in its short life   Forgiveness.

Things crop up or come back in spite of beauty

dregs of old arguments disappointments –

no matter how we clear it out the head-house of dust and droppings

forgiveness for some is a country too far away.

If we get there it's the letting down of trouble   it's feeling

the earth heal   one dark spot amended.

Tattoo

As I get older time prances his soldier

up and down the path,

I see him on the patio and wonder

can he see through glass?

I dread he might peer in

or slip a crack and enter

stand over me and grin, malevolently.

How do I know it's time

and not a random soul, a drifter, a homeless man

tortured by a dream he's had ?

Time tattooed a soldier's arm with hearts

the names of those he loved, an eagle.

The gun is real and the hand.

Wound

God of the young-old
console my ageing child, my progeria.

The book of words lies snug beneath
weekend newspapers.
Front cover: a young girl eyes alive to a future —
earth, dust, air...
her tiny scarlet nails:
droplets of ink she writes her life with.

I have had more time by far, so far.
I think I've crossed the same bridge
over and over —
same river, same blue pines rising
like fingers from icy water.

On waking
the garden's a baking-oven of birds
a chorus of joy,
life blood to a sad child —
the wound unrealized until now.

Flame

There's a fire burning on my desk.
I look out a window smeared with light
swallows weave through the glass   I watch
until their wing-beats resuscitate
the unspeakable heart.

Then I build an edifice   a house of myth
spooled by my own right-hand-left
the loom moving so fast
colours flame where they burn   smoulder
in skies   that widen   spread.
Everywhere I look small fires quench.

Storm

The sea comes faultless toward me

It has no deceit it never lies

It stays powerful element

Between me and your eyes.

The Lepidopterist

I would like to lie perfectly still
in a brown room
my completeness contained
in a slim elongated form.
I would like to have wings —
golden sails that fold around me.

Then as the sun rises
and the blue hills become
saturate with light
I would open my enormous wings
and fly from the brown room
toward a thin magenta light.

I Believe There Are Words Too Deep To Find
for John

Dark on long grass and a strong wind lashing the sand back.

Someone pulls the thread of the night in, bears its load.

The night's dream is light sleeping, as it does.

You wait, as if light would elicit singing

in your poor heart of sadness sister.

Always together the pull and

the tie, never tranquil, but

lenient as a mother

and shy.

Letters to an Immigrant Poet

for Magda

I

Take care your heart does not corrode

with the ire of the city.

I have lived there with its countless tongues

and its relentless hunger.

Don't be swallowed into the belly

of its utter requirements.

II

Trust me nothing is true

not even kindness which you cherish.

The city is a vortex of voices that cannot be heard

above the noise of machinery and alarms.

Their nascent terror rises.

III

Poets are ridiculed as they cling

to the railings of meaning.

They cry out to the river and walls

as if these would absorb feeling.

But stone and water will not bear witness.

IV

You were born in a foreign city

this is your badge you cannot remove it.

For a second I saw you as a child

but your eyes filled with years.

Sorrow enters the streets.

It sleeps in a corner covered with clothes

the ones you discarded –

garments of promise that kept out the cold.

V

Even now you slip like a shadow

between language and meaning.

They're waiting

to siphon the music from you.

I want to appeal to your mouth in snow

before it fills with whiteness.

Before ice grips it and that fragile warmth

the colour of cherries goes.

Cortona

For Dick

What scurries the undergrowth?
Quick silver shadow, criss-cross of shapes
glint of a long tail disappearing…

This morning the doves won't let up their calling.
Life of the immediate –
urgent display of wings shoot across the garden.

Who says Joy and sits among them
old hand turning a page –
the Book of Lost Things open on the table?

Circus Europe

The ringmaster watches from his closed interior –
every word he mouths dissolves against the glass.

He's watching us eat a breakfast of oats and ice.

The joker spread a virus of deceit –
he wears a shirker's mask and fills our fists with sweets.

I have photographs as proof:
caged radicals, a swinging moon and glitter sticks,
sequinned women trafficked from the east,

trumpets hooting, everything undoing
and someone at the centre singing –
Ode to Attempts at Unity.

Who are these two – freedom and unity or
unity and freedom?
Is that romantic or eternity?

And the fire-eater's cocky face –
his shaven head, his tongue aflame inside his throat,
his civility, the lies, the half-democracies he invents.

Where is food for thought of citizens?

Emigrants move from place to place, they carry blankets
and old songs. Two trains leave every hour
from Athens to Gare Saint-Lazare.

Look in the mirror – look in truth, but who saw what?
When the blocks fell down another hell popped up
this time of plaster and dust.

Old cities, old light, old monster buildings –
a woman swims beneath the lamps
like hope hopelessly in a trance.

I can't stop the dream that winter brings:
the carcass of a bird picked-clean
its wishbone a beam of light inside a vulture.

Snow is falling in Berlin.
In Mauerpark children walk their dogs.
City of dark nights, the Banks on Pariser Platz

are bright as vaulted churches.

Last Journey,

those words came to me like someone slipping in

through the back door of a cinema just as the film begins.

There he is   standing in the dark   unseen.

The air is suddenly heavy.

I smell cut-wood familiar as a work-shed full of father

and I'm watching people I've loved flit across the screen.

I realize I still love them.

I carry them around   they weigh in me

but they are blameless as shadows.

Then an interlude: a short movie about me. I'm holding a swan in my arms

it is large and cumbersome   oily as a fish.

I watch myself struggle with my awkwardness.

I'm waiting for the audience to laugh. Someone coughs at the back

of the cinema   it sounds like shame suddenly shook himself and left.

I'm looking into the swan's eyes   I'm surprised by their depth

and its beak is gnarled   the colour of silt and spilt egg.

Then it tips my lips with its beak   a kiss —

a tiny discharge bubbles between us.

A woman leans over   whispers in my ear. She insists

I leave immediately and go to The Clinic for Rare and Tropical Diseases.

I'm infected   she says.

I look up   the swan has gone and I'm alone in a waiting-room

listening to trains passing into darkness   to daylight   to darkness...

Today,

the day after the ninth day of August.

Year after year the ninth morning reoccurs

pale over the horizon.

We need someone to carry the complication

to raise it above us so we can walk unnoticed

at least in this life —

even if it's a lie that's ingrained

that's massive *(in this life)*

it gives comfort to a man or a child

or a woman   shivering

trying to make herself small

so she can be inside again —

in the interminable water   not-knowing

not-here   or there where she is now

in a burnt-out building

on a street in Aleppo   waiting

in our twenty-first century

for her life to begin…

Notes to Poems

Daughter Lucy: "Put Your Shoes on Lucy." Song composed in 1947 by Hank Fort and sung by the popular English vocalist, Anne Shelton (1923-1994.) "Show Me the Way to Go Home" written and recorded in 1925 by the songwriting duo, 'Irving King.'

Le Monde: A French daily newspaper.

The Picture of Inkbrush: Wei Shuo or Lady Wei (272-349 A.D.) was a calligrapher of Eastern Jin, who established consequential rules about regular script. The title is taken from the book, *The Picture of Ink Brush* by Lady Wei in which she describes the Seven Powers that became the famous Eight Principals of Yong.

The Artist's Room: The series of poems, The Artist's Room is based on the life and work of the painter Gwen John, (1876 – 1939). Gwen John is recognised as one of the finest and most influential painters of her generation. She was born in Haverfordwest, Wales and died in Dieppe, France, aged 63. She attended the Slade School of Fine Art, London. She worked as an artist's model and spent most of her working and painting life in Paris. During her years in Paris she lived at many different addresses, settling finally at 8 rue Babie Meudon, outside Paris. She modelled for Auguste Rodin and became his lover. She posed for the sculpture *The Whistler Muse*. After Rodin's death in 1917 she focused solely on her painting. She converted to Catholicism and led a life of devotion to her art.

Wound: Progeria. Hutchinson Gilford Progeria Syndrome is a rare genetic disease where symptoms resembling aspects of ageing are manifested at a very early age.

Today: On the ninth of August 1942, St. Edith Stein, philosopher and poet, was gassed at Auschwitz. On the ninth of August 1945, an atomic bomb was dropped on the city of Nagasaki, Japan, killing an estimated 60,000-80,000 people.

JO SLADE was born in Burkhamsted, Hertfordshire, England and educated in Limerick and Dublin. She is the author of four collections of poetry: *In Fields I Hear Them Sing* (Salmon Publishing 1989), *The Vigilant One* (Salmon Publishing 1994), which was nominated for the Irish Times/Aer Lingus Literature Prize; *Certain Octobers* (Editions Eireanna, Quimper France, 1997), a dual language English/French edition, which received a publication bursary from the Centre du Livre, Paris, France; and *City of Bridges* (Salmon Publishing 2005). A chapbook of poems, *The Artist's Room,* was published by Pighog Press, Brighton, UK in 2010. She was nominated in 2003 for the Prix Evelyn Encelot, Ecriture Prize, Maison des Ecrivains, Paris. Her poems have been translated into French, Spanish, Romanian, Russian and Slovenian. Her work has been published in journals and anthologies in Ireland and abroad. In 2002/2003 she was Poet-in-Residence for Limerick County Council and in 2007 she was Writer-in-Residence at the Centre Culturel Irlandais, Paris, France. She is a painter and has exhibited her paintings in Ireland and France.